Fraser Valley Elementary School

398.2 RUM
Pirotta, Saviour.   Guess my name : a Celtic fairy tale ;

T 3000267

⇥ ONCE UPON A WORLD ⇤

GUESS MY NAME
A Celtic Fairy Tale

and also
RUMPELSTILTSKIN

by SAVIOUR PIROTTA
and ALAN MARKS

SEA-TO-SEA
Mankato Collingwood London

This edition first published in 2008 by
Sea-to-Sea Publications
1980 Lookout Drive
North Mankato
Minnesota 56003

Text copyright © Saviour Pirotta 2004, 2008
Illustrations copyright © Alan Marks 2004

Printed in China

Library of Congress Cataloging-in-Publication Data

Pirotta, Saviour.
    Guess my name / by Saviour Pirotta and Alan Marks.
        p. cm. -- (Once upon a world)
    Summary: Presents two tales to compare and contrast, the first one from
Wales and the second one from Germany.
    ISBN 978-1-59771-082-4
    1. Fairy tales. [1. Fairy tales. 2. Folklore.] I. Marks, Alan, 1957- II. Title.

PZ8.P6672Gu 2007
[398.2]--dc22
                                                            2007060717

9 8 7 6 5 4 3 2

Published by arrangement with the Watts Publishing Group Ltd, London.

Editor: Rachel Cooke
Series design: Jonathan Hair

Contents

Once upon a time

Have you ever called a friend or relative by a special name no one else used? Or been upset when someone got your name wrong? Names can be very important to us and we have created many stories about them—*Rumpelstiltskin*, retold at the end of this book, is one of the most famous.

Fairy tales like *Rumpelstiltskin* were told and retold long before they were ever written down. They recall ancient beliefs, for example, the idea that names were much more than labels or ways to identify people, but were an actual part of the person, a key to their spirit.

The people of ancient Egypt had two names, known as the "big" name and the "little" name. They revealed the "little" name to everyone they knew, but the "big" name was a closely guarded

secret. Only trusted friends and family knew it, and they only used it on very special occasions. Other people around the world, such as Native Americans, also kept their real name secret. They believed that strangers, or evil spirits, could use their names to put a harmful spell on them.

No wonder, then, that there are so many myths, legends, and folktales about the importance of names. Some of the earliest ones appear in the sacred texts of ancient Egypt, as well as in the writings of ancient Rome. Many other cultures have tales where, as in *Rumpelstiltskin*, an ordinary person has to guess the name of a magic helper or fairy. There's a Caribbean story where the helper is a witch doctor called Granny Sogando, and an Eastern European one where the secret name is Kinkach Martinko. *Guess My Name*, which follows now, is set in Wales and is one of several Celtic tales based around this theme.

Guess My Name

Once there was a young farmer called Angwyn. His name meant handsome in Welsh, and handsome he was too; all the girls in the village were in love with him. Angwyn paid them no attention. He lived alone, working on his farm and fishing in the lake near his home.

One night, Angwyn happened to look out of the bedroom window and his eye was caught by something strange—lights flickering in the mist rising off the lake.

"There are strangers on my land," thought Angwyn. "I hope they're not after my sheep."

He put on a coat and went out
to chase away the intruders. Ahead
of him, the strange lights swooped and
soared, like dandelions blown around by
the wind. Angwyn began to feel more
than worried. He was scared.

Just then the mist cleared and he saw
them—not the strangers he was expecting,
but fairies!

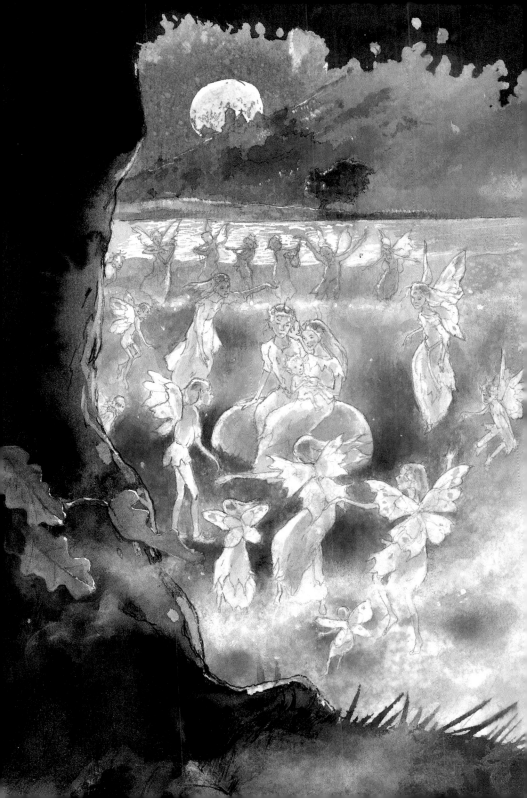

They were dancing
gracefully around a fairy
queen and king. The royal
couple were seated on a
moon-pale stone, the queen
feeding honey to a naked baby
on her lap. Bearded musicians
played lullabies on flutes and harps.
The lights Angwyn had seen were
moonbeams reflected on the fairies' wings.
He rubbed his eyes. Was he really seeing
this, or was he dreaming?

Entranced, Angwyn hid
behind a tree to watch.
One of the dancing
fairies seemed to him
more beautiful and
more graceful than the
rest. He couldn't take
his eyes off of her.

All too soon the cock crowed. It was dawn. The fairy king spread his wings and flew to the very tree behind which Angwyn was hiding. The king knocked on it three times. A door in the trunk swung open. The queen disappeared through it with her baby, followed by the rest of the fairies.

The fairy that had caught Angwyn's eye came last of all. The door was already swinging shut as she approached it. Angwyn leaped out and grabbed her by the arm. The fairy screamed and called for help. But it was too late. The sun had cleared the horizon and the door in the tree trunk vanished.

Knowing that sunlight was harmful to fairies, Angwyn threw his coat over his captive and carried her, kicking and screaming, to his farm.

He set her down in an old chair but she jumped up immediately. "Let me go, mortal," she hissed. "My friends will come looking for me."

Even hissing and spitting, the fairy looked magnificent. In a moment Angwyn knew he could never be content with anyone else.

He fell to his knees. "Be my wife," he said.

The fairy laughed cruelly. "Marry you? A farmer! A mortal! Never!"

"Then you shall stay here as my prisoner," said Angwyn, climbing to his feet. "You cannot escape, even when the sun sets. The windows have iron locks on them and fairies cannot touch iron. It's as harmful to them as sunshine."

The fairy bristled with rage at Angwyn's words but she knew that she was trapped. "I'll make a bargain with you, mortal. If you

can guess my name by midnight in a week's time, I shall remain here as your servant. But, if you fail, you must let me go back to my queen."

"How do I know you'll keep your word if I guess your name?" asked Angwyn.

The fairy looked at him with contempt. "A fairy always keeps her promise, even to a mortal," she sneered.

"Then I accept your bargain," said Angwyn. He made sure that the windows in the cottage were properly bolted and left the house, locking the door behind him. All day long he sat on the shores of the lake, racking his brains. By night-time his head was spinning, but he'd thought of a hundred names.

"Are you called Alis?" he asked the fairy when he got back home. "Is your name Bethan or Crisiant?"

The fairy shook her head at every name he gave, and her translucent wings quivered in defiance. "It is not. It is not."

"I'm not defeated yet," thought Angwyn. "I still have six days to go."

The next morning he was up before dawn.
Again he made sure that the windows were
properly bolted and left the house, locking
the door behind him. This time he went to
the church in the village. All day long he
sat behind the altar, reading the names in
the parish register. By night time he was
exhausted but he'd learnt two hundred
more names.

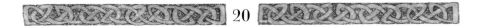

"Are you called Delyth?" he asked the fairy when he returned home. "Is your name Fflur? Or Gwen? Could it be Hafina? Is it Sîan?"

Again, the fairy shook her head at every name. "It is not. It is not."

"I must not lose heart," the young farmer told himself as he tried to sleep that night. "I still have five more days to go."

The next morning he got up even earlier.
As usual, he made sure the windows were
properly bolted and the door locked. Then
he saddled his mare and rode out. For the
next four days Angwyn traveled from town
to town, collecting names. On the sixth
morning he reached the city of Carnavon.

He wandered around the market, asking
every woman and girl he met: "What is
your name? Pray, tell me your name." It was
late by the time he set out for home. He
rode through the night across the hills,
feeling more tired than he'd ever been in his
life, but he knew five hundred more names.

"Are you Megan?" he asked the fairy. "Is your name Gwyneth or Marion?"

Once more she shook her head at every name. "It is not. It is not."

Across the lake, the church clock chimed the hour. Eleven o'clock! "One hour to go," thought Angwyn desperately. "What shall I do now?"

He went down to the lake to think. Almost at once he became aware of an angry buzzing, like bees around a hive. He hid behind a bush and, through its branches, spied an army of fairies. The rabble was bristling with spears. The fairy king was at its helm: "Follow me," he cried, "we shall find the mortal's house and rescue Penelop."

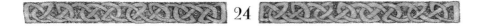

The rabble cheered and, waving its weapons, moved forward, passing right by Angwyn's hiding place.

"Penelop! That must be the fairy's name," thought Angwyn. He stood up and bolted toward his farm, praying he would get there before the fairy army.

The church clock began to strike twelve as Angwyn opened the farm house door. "Are you called Tanwen?" he asked the fairy. "Is your name Undeg or Valmai?"

"It is not. It is not." She spread her wings, ready to fly.

"Wait a second," said Angwyn. "Your name is Penelop."

Taken by surprise, the fairy gasped. "It is."

"Pe-ne-lop."

Hearing her name again, Penelop shrieked in pain. She swooped from window to window, crashing into the glass like a trapped bird. But nothing, not even the fairy army, could save her now. She was Angwyn's servant, forever, for a fairy can never break her promise.

At last the poor creature sank to the floor,
defeated. Her wings trembled and, as
Angwyn watched, they grew more and
more transparent until they were there no
more. With her name revealed, the fairy had
lost her powers.

Even with all her magic gone, Penelop
was still the most beautiful woman Angwyn
had ever seen. He didn't want her to be his
servant. He wanted her to share his life.

"Be my wife," he begged and cajoled her, day in, day out. "Marry me. We'll be happy."

At last she said, "Very well, I'll marry you, but, as always, there is one condition. If you ever touch me with iron, I shall return to my people."

"That's a condition I'll gladly accept," said Angwyn, and he picked up Penelop and swung her around in delight.

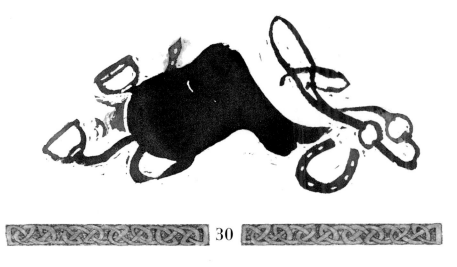

Angwyn set out to get rid of every scrap of iron in the house. The metal pots and pans were replaced with clay ones. Knives and forks, pails and spoons, thimbles and needles—all were thrown to the bottom of the lake, to rust out of harm's way. The mare's saddle and bridle, which had iron stirrups and bit, Angwyn locked in the shed, where only he could get to them.

A year after the wedding, Penelop bore twins, a boy and a girl. As she fed them one night, Angwyn became concerned: "The girl is coughing. I should fetch the doctor. I'll go on the mare."

"Take your scarf," said Penelop. "It's cold and misty tonight."

Angwyn, hurrying out, did not hear her. He fetched the saddle from the shed and took it to the stable.

The mare, unable to see him in the mist, neighed nervously. "Stand still," said Angwyn. He threw the saddle over her back but she moved and he missed.

"Stand still, I tell you." Again, Angwyn threw the saddle and missed.

"I beg
you, stand
still." A third
time he threw the
saddle.

This time he heard a gasp
in the mist. He looked up and
saw Penelop holding out his scarf.
She had followed him. Blood was
trickling out of a gash on her cheek.
He'd hit her with the iron stirrup.

"Penelop," he cried out.

She looked back at him with the same pain he'd seen on her face the night he'd guessed her name. All around her lights appeared, moonbeams reflecting on a thousand fairies' wings. Her own wings reappeared, unfolding like a new dragonfly's.

"Penelop," he screamed, "don't go. I didn't mean to hit you. It was an accident."

Even before the king and queen appeared to take her by the hands, even before the fairy army closed in around her and she was gone from sight, leaving his scarf on the ground, he knew he had lost her.

Angwyn searched all over the countryside for his fairy wife, to no avail. He even looked for the door in the tree, hoping to enter the fairies' underground lair and rescue his beloved, but he never found it. And even if he did find Penelop, Angwyn knew she would never be allowed to come back to him. She was a fairy after all, and a fairy can never break her promise, not even to a mortal.

With Penelop gone, Angwyn could no longer sleep. Every night he lay awake in bed, the babies close beside him, wishing she could see how quickly they were growing. The children were restless, too, crying and whimpering in their sleep.

Then one night a loud noise made him jump. The wind had blown the window open. Angwyn leaned out to close it again and what did he see? Strange lights flickering in the mist rising off the lake. And he heard music:

"Lest my son should find it cold
Place on him his father's coat;
Lest the fair one find it cold
Place on her my petticoat."

It was Penelop, singing a
lullaby to her children. He
couldn't see her but she was there.
She hadn't forgotten him or her
children after all. She was still a part of the
family. Tears of joy welled in Angwyn's
eyes. "Penelop," he whispered as the lights
started to fade, "I love you."

And then he got into his bed, and he and
the children slept peacefully for the first
time since Penelop had disappeared.

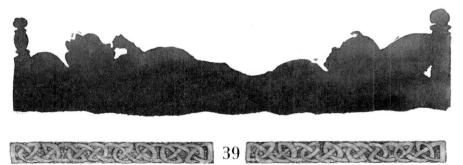

Rumpelstiltskin

Rumpelstiltskin is one of the most popular stories collected by the famous brothers Grimm. They wrote down stories they heard told aloud by German farmworkers—stories that had been passed down by word of mouth for generations. This retelling is based on the last of four versions they recorded, published in 1857.

Once there was a miller who had a beautiful daughter. He was poor but he couldn't help boasting. One day he met the king and he got so carried away showing off, that he said, "My daughter can spin straw into gold."

"I love gold," said the king. "Send your daughter to my palace at once."

That very night the miller's girl was taken to the palace. The king showed her into a small room full of straw. There was a spinning wheel in the corner, with a little stool right next to it.

The king said, "Start
spinning, and if by morning
you haven't spun all this
straw into gold, I shall have
you put to death." Then he
locked the door and went away.

The miller's daughter sat on the stool and
stared at the spinning wheel. She had no
idea how to spin straw into gold. "What am
I going to do?" she cried.

Suddenly the door creaked
open and a little man tiptoed
in. He was very thin, with
long fingers. "Good evening,"
he said, "why are you crying?"
"I have to spin all this straw
into gold," said the girl,
"but I don't know how to do it."
"What will you give me if I
spin it for you?" asked the man.
"My necklace," said the girl.

The little man took the necklace, then he sat down at the spinning wheel and started spinning. Whirr! Whirr! Whirr! He worked so fast, the girl could hardly see his fingers moving. By morning all the straw had disappeared and in its place were heaps of spun gold. The little man bid her good day and quietly left.

A little later the girl heard the key turn in the lock and the king came in. When he saw the gold, his eyes shone with greed. He took the girl to a bigger room, also piled high with straw. "Weave that into gold," he ordered, "or I shall have you put to death."

Once again the girl could only weep, and once again, as night fell, the door creaked open and in tiptoed the little man.

 "What will you give me if I spin the straw into gold again for you?" he asked.

"The ring from my finger," replied the girl.

The little man took the ring and started spinning. Whirr! Whirr! Whirr! Working even faster than before, by morning he had spun all the straw into glistening gold.

The king was delighted when he saw it. He took the miller's daughter to the biggest room in the palace, piled right up to the ceiling with straw. "Spin all this into gold," he ordered, "and I shall marry you. Fail me, and both you and your father will die."

Once more the girl sat crying until midnight, when the little man appeared. "What will you give me if I spin the straw this time?"

"I have nothing left to give you," answered the girl.

"Then promise me that, if you become queen, you will give me your first child," said the man.

"The king will never marry a miller's daughter anyway," thought the girl. And she promised the little man what he wanted. In return he once again spun the straw into gold, bid the girl good morning and left just as mysteriously as he had arrived.

But the king kept his word. He married the miller's daughter and the humble girl became a queen.

A few years later the queen had a baby son, whom she loved more than anything.

One night, just after the christening, the door to her chamber creaked open and in walked the little man with long fingers.

"I have come for the child," he said.

The queen hugged the baby close. "I cannot give you my child," she cried. "I'll give you anything else—treasure, a palace, a part of the kingdom even." She cried so hard that the little man had pity on her. "If in three days' time, you know my name," he said, "you shall keep your child."

The queen spent all night thinking of names. When the little man returned the next day she said, "Is your name Kaspar, or Melchior, or Balthasar?" At each name, the little man said, "No, that's not what I'm called."

The next day, the queen sent her servants to gather names and, when the little man appeared, she recited the most unusual ones they had found. "Is your name Beansprout? Or Muttoncalf? Or Hamstring?" But the man always answered, "It is not."

On the third day, a servant came to the queen. "Yesterday, I found myself in a far corner of the woods," he said. "There I saw a little house. A fire was burning outside it, and a strange man with long fingers was leaping over the flames and singing:

"Today I'll bake; tomorrow I'll brew,
Then I'll fetch the queen's new child.
I'm so lucky no one knows that my name is Rumpelstiltskin."

A little later the man came to the queen and asked. "Your highness,

what is my name?'

The queen pretended to hesitate. "Is your name Kunz?"

"No."

"Is your name Hans?"

"No."

"Then is your name, perhaps, Rumpelstiltskin?"

"The devil told you that," screamed the little man. He was so angry that he started stamping his feet and his right foot went through the floorboards. Rumpelstiltskin grabbed his left foot in both hands and tried to pull himself free. He pulled so hard that he ripped himself in two— and that was the end of that!

Taking it further

Once you've read both stories in this book, there is lots more you can think and talk about. There's plenty to write about, too.

• To begin with, think about what is the same and what is different about the two stories. Talk about these with other people. Which story do you prefer and why? Does either story remind you of any other famous fairytales?

• Do you or your friends have a middle name? Try to guess each other's middle name in twenty questions. Don't just suggest names, think of other questions that might help you guess.

• Write a story set in the real world, rather than a fairytale one, where someone has to find out another person's name. Perhaps the mystery person could be a spy or a stranger who's helped the other person get out of a dangerous situation.

• Try writing a play based on one of the stories— or a part of it. Which part would you like to play, the magic creature or the mortal?